The Complete Baking Cookbook for Young Chefs

115 Amazing & Delicious Recipes for Young Bakers to Learn the Baking Basics

Charles Gutfranski

April Mays

Table of Contents

Chapter 1: Cakes Recipes..**8**

Cinnamon Coffee Cake 8

Berry Cake 8

Strawberry Cheesecake 9

White Cake 10

Blueberry Shortcake 10

Banana Split Cake 11

Pink Velvet Cake 12

Elegant Tea Cakes 13

Cherry Cheesecake 14

Birthday Cake 14

Vanilla (Yellow) Cake 15

Shortcake 16

Butterscotch Trifle Cake 16

Banana Cream Cake 17

Strawberry Cake 18

Snowman Cake 18

Carrot Cake 19

Chocolate Cake 20

Orange Nut Cake 20

Peanut Butter Cake 21

Crazy Cake 22

Vanilla (Yellow) Cake Mix 23

Strawberry Shortcake 23

Chocolate Cake 24

Chapter 2: Cookies Recipes **25**

Cake Batter Cookies (from box mix) 25

Peanut Butter & Chocolate Spirals (cookie dough) 26

Fruity Fingers (from refrigerated cookie dough) 27

Chocolate Chip Cookies (from box cake mix) 27

Edible Hands (from refrigerated cookie dough) 28

Peanut Butter Cookie Cups (from cookie dough) 29

Cake Batter Peanut Butter Cookies (from box mix) 29

Cookie Pops (from refrigerated cookie dough) 30

Chocolate Cookies (from mug mix) 31

Yummy Cookie Butter Cookies (from scratch) 31

Chocolate Peanut Butter Sandwich Cookies 32

Lady Finger Cookies (from scratch) 33

Chocolate Peanut Butter Cookies (from box mix) 34

Strawberry Cups (from refrigerated cookie dough) 34

Chocolate Peanut Butter Cups (cookie dough) 35

Basic Sandwich Cookies (from refrigerated dough) 36

Birthday Cake Cookies (from box mix) 37

Chapter 3: Glazings and Frostings Recipes **38**

Crystal Sugar Frosting 38

Lemon Frosting 38

Strawberry Frosting 39

Garlic Glaze 39

Cream Cheese Frosting 40

Peppermint Frosting 40

Vanilla Frosting #1 41

Vanilla Frosting #2 41

Buttercream Frosting 42

Peanut Butter Frosting 42

Watermelon Frosting.. 43

Orange Glaze 44

White Frosting 44

Chocolate Frosting... 45

Sparkling Frosting 46

Chapter 4: Main Course Baking Recipes **47**

Lasagna 47

Chicken Pot Pie 48

Baked Ziti 50

Chicken Fiesta Bake... 51

Pizza 52

Shepherd's Pie 53

Roasted Whole Chicken with Root Vegetables 55

Meatloaf... 56

Chicken & Rice Casserole 58

Baked Macaroni and Cheese... 59

Chapter 5: Bars Recipes **61**

Raspberry Bars 61

Oatmeal Fruit Bars 62

Granola Bars... 62

Apple Bar 63

6-Layer Bar 64

Chocolate Peanut Butter Bars 65

Chapter 6: Brownies Recipes **66**

Brownies Mix #1 66

Brownies Mix #2 67

Mint Chocolate Brownies.. 67

Graham Brownie Mix 68

Double Fudge Brownies 69

Chapter 7: Baked Snack Recipes **70**

Banana Bread 70

Smoky Pretzel Mix 71

Almond-Raisin Granola 72

Lemon Raspberry Muffins 73

Pizza Pockets 74

Cheddar Biscuits 76

Zucchini Bread 77

Blueberry Pound Cake 78

Jam Pockets 79

Croissants 80

Chapter 8: Baked Dessert Recipes **82**

Chocolate Cake 82

Blondies.. 83

Carrot Cake 84

Chocolate Chip Cookies 86

Apple Pie.. 87

Snickerdoodles.. 88

Coffee Cake 89

Cheesecake 91

Lemon Bars 92

NOTE TO PARENTS / GUARDIANS:

Adult assistance required for safety and sanitary purposes

Welcome to the Hasty Tasty family! We love having fun with all of the Chef's that join us and we're so glad you're here!

Are you wanting to cook something sweet? How about something savory? It doesn't matter if you want cake, brownies or cookies or maybe even pizza and bread sticks. You can find it all in your new cookbook.

Do you want something you can whip up in a minute? You can surely do this by creating a "semi" homemade cake. You simply start with a cake mix base from a box! Easy Peasy! We've got lots and lots of recipes for you to choose from.

There may also be times you want to make everything from scratch. Honestly, that doesn't happen quiet as much in our kitchen, but on a rare occasion, it does happen. Because we want you to have what you need, your new cookbook also includes several "from scratch" recipes that you can enjoy!

Here are a few Tips for Success that we hope will help:

When a recipe calls for all-purpose flour, we like to use White Lily™ brand for a fluffy and light cake. We also use cake flour if we are out of White Lily. You can use whatever you have access to. We just wanted to share what works for us.

Always preheat your oven before mixing the ingredients for the cake.

Quick Tip: Want to cook more than one cake at a time or test out a recipe? Your EASY-BAKE oven cooks at about 350 degrees F. You can easily set your regular oven to the same temperature and use it to test out your recipes or to cook multiple items at once. Please follow all safety precautions.

Cooking Brownies: Brownies will continue to cook a little even after you pull them out of the oven. They will not look done like your cakes will. Always test your brownies by inserting a clean toothpick into the center and removing to check for uncooked batter on the toothpick. Check frequently to ensure that you do not overcook your brownies.

Chapter 1: Cakes Recipes

Cinnamon Coffee Cake

Ingredients:

- 1/3 cup biscuit mix (such as Bisquick)

- 2 3/4 teaspoons white sugar

- 1 teaspoon butter

- 1/2 teaspoon of a slightly beaten egg

- 1/4 teaspoon cinnamon

- 1 tablespoon milk

Directions:

1. Stir all ingredients together until just moistened.

2. Pour into greased and floured oven pan.

3. Bake for 15 minutes. Let cool.

Berry Cake

Ingredients:

- 4 yellow cakes (see Yellow Cake page)

- 1/4 cup heavy, liquid whipping cream

- 1/3 cup blueberries

- 2 strawberries

- Cake Mate decorating gel tubes; optional

Directions:

1. Bake 4 yellow cake layers per directions and let cool.

2. Whip heavy whipping cream with 2 teaspoons of sugar until it holds soft peaks.

3. Place one cake layer on cake plate.

4. Spread 1/4 of prepared whipped cream on the layer.

5. Top with 8 blueberries around edge of cake and 1 blueberry in center.

6. Place second cake layer on top of first.

7. Spread 1/4 of prepared whipped cream on cake.

8. Top with 8 blueberries around edge of cake and 1 blueberry in center.

9. Place third cake layer on top of second.

10. Spread 1/4 of prepared whipped cream on third layer.

11. Top with 8 blueberries around edge of cake and 1 strawberry in center.

12. Place remaining cake on top of third.

13. Spread remaining whipped cream on fourth cake layer.

14. Top with 8 blueberries around edge of cake

15. Top with 1 strawberry in the center.

16. Create designs on top of cake and around berries using decorating gel.

Makes one 4-Layer Cake

Strawberry Cheesecake

Ingredients:

* 1 batch sugar cookie dough, prepared as directed (see sugar cookies)

For Cream Cheese filling

* 2 tablespoons cream cheese

* 2 teaspoons confectioners' sugar

* 2 tablespoons strawberry pie filling

Directions:

1. Press cookie dough evenly into oven pan.

2. Bake for 15 - 20 minutes, until golden brown.

3. Cool in pan on wire rack.

4. Mix together cream cheese, confectioners' sugar and pie filling.

5. Spread cream cheese filling on cooled cheesecake.

6. Cover with strawberry pie filling.

White Cake

Ingredients:

- 1/4 cup of boxed white cake mix

- 2 tablespoons water

Directions:

1. Preheat your oven for 20 minutes.

2. Lightly coat the oven pan with butter.

3. When the oven has heated, pour the 1/4 cup of mix into a bowl.

4. Add 2 tablespoons of water.

5. Mix thoroughly.

6. Spread the cake mix evenly in the pan.

7. Bake for 16-18 minutes.

8. Remove from oven and cool for 5 minutes.

9. Spread frosting of your choice on the cake.

10. Decorate with sprinkles or other cake decorations.

Blueberry Shortcake

Ingredients:

- 1/4 cup biscuit mix

- 5 teaspoons milk

- Blueberries

- 1 tablespoon sugar

- 1/8 teaspoon cinnamon

- Whipped cream

Directions:

1. In a bowl, combine the biscuit mix and milk, using a fork.

2. Divide into two portions.

3. Roll one at a time on a floured surface to fit a pan.

4. Place each roll in a buttered pan.

5. Bake about 10 minutes.

6. Let cool and transfer to a clean bowl.

7. In a separate bowl, combine the blueberries, sugar and cinnamon.

8. Pour the blueberry mixture over the cake.

9. Top with the whipped cream.

Banana Split Cake

Ingredients:

- 1 yellow cake mix

- 5 tablespoons fruit cocktail syrup

- 1 small banana

- 3 teaspoons vanilla ice cream

- 1 tablespoon each of pineapple syrup, strawberry syrup, and chocolate syrup

- Whipped cream

- 1 cherry

- Pecan or walnut pieces

Directions:

1. Stir cake mix and fruit cocktail syrup together until well blended and smooth.

2. Pour batter into a round, buttered cake pan.

3. Bake for 18 - 20 minutes or until cake is done.

4. Slice cooled cake in half to make two, even, round cake layers.

5. Place banana halves on bottom layer of cake, & trim overhanging pieces.

6. Place 3, 1-tablespoon scoops of ice cream across the banana halves.

7. Top each scoop with a different topping (pineapple, strawberry, chocolate syrup).

8. Add the top layer of cake.

9. Garnish the top of the cake with whipped cream, cherry and nut pieces.

10. Decorate your cake plate with ice cream toppings.

Pink Velvet Cake

Ingredients:

- 5 tablespoons flour

- 1/4 teaspoon baking powder

- 1/8 teaspoon salt

- 5 teaspoons red sugar crystals

- 1/4 teaspoon vanilla

- 4 teaspoons butter

- 8 teaspoons milk

Directions:

1. Stir together all ingredients until batter is smooth and pink.

2. Pour 3 tablespoons of batter into greased and floured cake pan.

3. Bake 15 minutes.

4. Repeat for second layer.

5. Optional; frost with frosting of your choice.

Suggested Frostings:

Sparkling frosting

Strawberry frosting

White frosting with a drop of red food coloring

Makes 2 Layers

Elegant Tea Cakes

Ingredients:

*   1/4 cup all-purpose flour

*   1/4 teaspoon baking powder

*   1/8 teaspoon salt

*   2 teaspoons sugar

*   2 teaspoons butter

*   4 teaspoons milk

*   1 teaspoon multi-colored cookie decorations

Directions:

1. Mix together flour, baking powder, salt, sugar and butter until dough looks like medium-sized crumbs.

2. Slowly mix in the milk to create dough.

3. Form the dough into a loose ball and divide it into 4 pieces.

4. Place the dough pieces on a greased sheet or pan.

5. Sprinkle the decorations over the dough.

6. Push the decorations into the dough with your fingers.

7. Bake 20 minutes.

Makes 4 tea cakes

Cherry Cheesecake

Ingredients:

- 1 sugar cookie dough, prepared
- 2 tablespoons cherry pie filling

Cream Cheese Filling

- 2 tablespoons cream cheese
- 2 teaspoons confectioners' sugar

irections:

1. Press cookie dough evenly into prepared pan.
2. Bake for 15 - 20 minutes, until golden brown.
3. Cool in pan on wire rack.
4. In large mixing bowl, mix cream cheese with confectioners' sugar.
5. Spread cream cheese filling on cooled cookie dough.
6. Cover with cherry pie filling.

Birthday Cake

Ingredients:

- 4 teaspoons flour
- 2 teaspoons cocoa powder
- 1 tablespoon sugar
- 1/8 teaspoon baking powder
- 1 dash salt

- 1/8 teaspoon vanilla

- 4 teaspoons water

- 2 teaspoons vegetable oil

- Frosting of your choice

Directions:

1. Combine all ingredients except frosting in a small bowl.

2. Stir until the batter is smooth and chocolate colored.

3. Pour the batter into a buttered and floured cake pan.

4. Bake for 13 to 15 minutes or until the cake pulls away from the sides of the pan.

5. Remove cake from oven and cool.

6. Cover with a frosting of your choice.

Makes 1 Layer

Vanilla (Yellow) Cake

Ingredients:

- 1/4 cup of boxed vanilla (or French vanilla) cake mix

- 2 tablespoons water

Directions:

1. Preheat your oven for 20 minutes.

2. Lightly coat the oven pan with butter.

3. When the oven has heated, pour the 1/4 cup of mix into a bowl.

4. Add 2 tablespoons of water.

5. Mix thoroughly.

6. Spread the cake mix evenly in the pan.

7. Bake for 16-18 minutes.

8. Remove from oven and cool for 5 minutes.

9. Spread frosting of your choice on the cake.

10. Decorate with sprinkles or other cake decorations.

Shortcake

Ingredients:

- 1/4 cup biscuit mix (Bisquick)

- 5 teaspoons milk

Directions:

1. Combine biscuit mix and milk using a fork.

2. Divide into two portions.

3. Roll one portion at a time on a floured surface to fit pan.

4. Place each portion in a greased pan.

5. Bake about 10 minutes.

6. Allow to cool.

Butterscotch Trifle Cake

Ingredients:

- 6 tablespoons boxed yellow cake mix (such as Duncan Hines)

- 2 tablespoons milk

- 4 tablespoons butterscotch pudding

- 3 tablespoons whipped cream

Directions:

1. Mix the yellow cake mix with 2 tablespoons of milk until smooth.

2. Bake in 2 prepared round cake pans for 15 minutes each.

3. Let cool.

4. Cut into small squares.

5. Fold pudding and whipped cream together.

6. In trifle dish or glass bowl arrange pieces from one cake in bottom.

7. Cover with pudding mixture.

8. Repeat.

9. Chill until served.

Makes 2 servings

Banana Cream Cake

Ingredients:

- 6 tablespoons flour

- 4 teaspoons sugar

- 1/4 teaspoon baking powder

- Dash salt

- 6 teaspoons milk

- 2 teaspoons butter

- Frosting of choice

- 3 tablespoons banana cream pudding mix

Directions:

1. Mix flour, sugar, baking powder and salt.

2. Add milk and butter.

3. Stir until batter is smooth

4. Add banana cream pudding mix.

5. Pour the batter into a buttered and floured oven pan.

6. Bake for 12 to 15 minutes or until sides of cake separates from pan.

7. Remove and cool.

Makes 2 Layers

Strawberry Cake

Ingredients:

- 1 package yellow cake mix or 1/2 cup boxed cake mix

- 2 teaspoons strawberry Jell-O powder

- 2 tablespoons milk

Directions:

1. Butter and flour two oven pans.

2. Combine all ingredients, stirring until batter is smooth.

3. Pour into prepared pans.

4. Bake for 12 to 15 minutes or until sides separate from pan.

5. Remove and cool.

6. Frost with strawberry frosting.

Snowman Cake

Ingredients:

- Enough pre-made white cakes mixes for 3 layers (or 3/4 cup boxed cake mix)

- 1/2 cup white frosting mix

- Mini marshmallows

- Red licorice

- Chocolate kisses

- Mini chocolate chips

- Gummy worms

- Coconut flakes

Directions:

1. Bake and cool 3 layers of round cake.

2. Arrange layers side-by-side on a plate to make a snowman shape.

3. Layer with white frosting.

4. Arrange marshmallows to cover the surface of each layer.

5. Use mini chocolate chips for eyes, nose and mouth.

6. Cut red licorice for a scarf

7. Use gummy worms for arms.

8. Sprinkle coconut flakes for "snow".

Carrot Cake

Ingredients:

- 2 yellow cake mixes

- 1/8 teaspoon ground cinnamon

- 2 pinches ground nutmeg

- 2 pinches ground ginger

- 1 tablespoon shredded carrots

- 2 teaspoons drained, crushed pineapple

- 1 teaspoon of a beaten egg

- 2 1/2 teaspoons water

- Cream cheese frosting

Directions:

1. Butter and flour 2 pans.

2. Combine all ingredients except frosting until completely mixed.

3. Pour 1/2 of mix into each pan.

4. Bake cakes for 9 – 11 minutes each.

5. Remove from pan and allow to cool.

6. Apply cream cheese frosting between layers, top and around cake.

Chocolate Cake

(from scratch)

Ingredients:

- 6 teaspoons flour

- 4 teaspoons sugar

- 1/4 teaspoon baking powder

- 1 teaspoon unsweetened cocoa

- 1 pinch salt

- 3/4 teaspoon butter

- 6 teaspoons milk

Directions:

1. Mix all dry ingredients

2. Slowly add milk and butter, mixing until smooth.

3. Pour into a greased baking pan.

4. Bake 15 minutes.

Makes 1 serving

Orange Nut Cake

Ingredients:

- 1/2 cup white cake mix (such as Duncan Hines)

- 1 teaspoon orange zest

- 4 tablespoons water

- 1/2 tablespoon chopped pecans

- 1/2 tablespoon coconut

- Orange glaze

Directions:

1. Mix 1/4 cup white cake mix with 1/2 teaspoon of orange zest and 2 tablespoons water.

2. Bake for 12 minutes in prepared round cake pan.

3. While the first cake layer is baking, prepare an orange glaze and set aside.

4. Remove first pan from oven and invert onto a small plate.

5. Mix the remaining white cake mix with remaining orange zest and water.

6. Bake for 12 minutes in another prepared round cake pan.

7. Pierce first layer with fork several times to help absorb the glaze.

8. Drizzle 1 1/2 teaspoons of the orange glaze over the top of the first layer.

9. Place second layer on first layer and drizzle remaining orange glaze over all.

10. Sprinkle the finished cake with nuts and coconut.

Peanut Butter Cake

Ingredients:

- 1 yellow cake mix (or 1/4 cup boxed vanilla cake mix)

- 1 tablespoon peanut butter

- 2 tablespoons milk

Directions:

1. Prepare two oven pans.

2. Combine all ingredients, stirring until batter is smooth.

3. Pour into prepared pans.

4. Bake for 12 to 15 minutes or until sides separate from pan.

5. Remove and cool.

6. Cover with frosting of your choice.

Make 2 cakes, or 1 double layer cake

Crazy Cake

Ingredients:

- 4 1/2 teaspoon flour

- 3 teaspoon sugar

- 1/4 teaspoon cocoa

- 1 dash salt

- 1/8 teaspoon baking soda

- 1 1/2 teaspoon butter

- 1/8 teaspoon vanilla

- 1/8 teaspoon vinegar

- 1 tablespoon water

Directions:

1. Mix the 5 dry ingredients together.

2. Add the 4 wet ingredients one at a time, stirring gently until mixed thoroughly.

3. Bake in oven about 10 minutes.

Vanilla (Yellow) Cake Mix

(from scratch)

Ingredients:

- 6 teaspoons flour

- 4 teaspoons sugar

- 1/4 teaspoon baking powder

- 1 pinch salt

- 3/4 teaspoon butter

- 6 teaspoons milk

- 2 drops of vanilla

Directions:

5. Mix all dry ingredients

6. Slowly add milk and butter, mixing until smooth.

7. Pour into a greased baking pan.

8. Bake 15 minutes.

Makes 1 serving

Strawberry Shortcake

Ingredients:

- 1/4 cup biscuit mix (Biscuick)

- 5 teaspoons milk

- Strawberries

- Whipped cream

Directions:

1. Combine biscuit mix and milk using a fork.

2. Divide into two portions.

3. Roll one at a time on a floured surface to fit pan.

4. Place each in a prepared pan.

5. Bake about 10 minutes or until golden brown.

6. Let cool.

7. Place in a bowl, top with strawberries and whipped cream

Chocolate Cake

Ingredients:

- 1/4 cup of boxed chocolate cake mix

- 2 tablespoons water

Directions:

1. Lightly coat an oven pan with butter.

2. Combine the cake mix and water.

3. Mix thoroughly.

4. Spread evenly in the pan.

5. Bake for 16 - 18 minutes.

6. Remove from oven and cool for 5 minutes.

7. Spread frosting of your choice on the cake.

8. Decorate with sprinkles or other cake decorations.

Chapter 2: Cookies Recipes

Cake Batter Cookies (from box mix)

Ingredients (cookies):

- 4 tablespoons white cake mix

- 4 tablespoons Betty Crocker ™ sugar cookie mix from pouch

- 1 tablespoon butter (melted)

- 1 ½ tablespoons applesauce or beaten egg

- 1/8 teaspoon vanilla extract

- ½ tablespoon sprinkles

Icing:

- 1 tablespoon butter (softened)

- 6 tablespoons powdered sugar

- 1 – 1 ½ teaspoons milk

- 1/8 teaspoon vanilla extract

- Sprinkles

Directions:

1. Preheat oven. Spray pans with nonstick spray

2. Mix all cookie ingredients together well

3. Roll cookies into balls and place on pan

4. Flatten cookies below the top level of the pan

5. Cook for approximately 10 minutes

6. Remove from oven and top with sprinkles

Peanut Butter & Chocolate Spirals (cookie dough)

Ingredients (cookies):

- Refrigerated chocolate cookie dough (1/8 of roll)

- Refrigerated peanut butter cookie dough (1/8 of roll)

- 1 ½ teaspoons semi-sweet chocolate chips

- 1 ½ teaspoons peanut butter flavored chips

- ¼ teaspoon all purpose flour

Directions:

1. Remove cookie dough from wrapper. Refrigerate remaining dough

2. Mix together chocolate cookie dough and peanut butter chips. Set aside

3. Mix together peanut butter cookie dough and flour. Add chocolate chips

4. Place both doughs in refrigerator for 1 hour

5. On a floured surface, roll each dough out into a rectangle about 1/8 to ¼ inch thick. You will have one chocolate and one peanut butter rectangle.

6. Place the peanut butter rectangle on top of the chocolate rectangle. Roll up dough to form a "cookie" roll (similar to a pumpkin roll)

7. Refrigerate for 1 additional hour

8. Preheat oven and spray pans with nonstick spray

9. Remove cookie roll from refrigerator and cut into ¼ to ½ inch slices

10. Place on greased pan and bake 10 -12 minutes until just slightly browned.

11. Remove and allow cookies to cool completely

Tip: Get creative! Mix and match any two flavors of refrigerated cookie dough to make it your own. Instead of chocolate and peanut butter chips, try other mix in's that you really like!

Fruity Fingers (from refrigerated cookie dough)

Ingredients (cookies):

- Refrigerated sugar cookie dough

- ½ cup crushed Fruit flavored cereal (divided)

Directions:

1. Remove desired amount of cookie dough from wrapper (depending on how many cookies you want to make). Refrigerate remaining dough

2. Mix together 1 teaspoon crushed cereal and cookie dough

3. Roll dough into balls and refrigerate for 1 hour

4. Preheat oven and spray pans with nonstick spray

5. Roll cookie balls into 2-3 inch long "fingers" (ropes)

6. Coat cookies by rolling in cereal

7. Place cookies on sheet making sure to leave enough room between them (1-2 inches)

8. Bake until just slightly brown (usually 8-10 minutes)

9. Remove and allow cookies to cool completely

Tip: I used the spatula to gently "shape" cookies while still warm

Chocolate Chip Cookies (from box cake mix)

Ingredients:

- 4 tablespoons yellow cake mix

- 1 tablespoon egg (beaten) or applesauce

- ½ teaspoon vanilla extract

- ¾ tablespoon butter (softened)

- 4 tablespoons semi- sweet chocolate chips

Directions:

1. Preheat oven. Spray pans with nonstick spray

2. Mix ingredients together in small bowl

3. Roll cookie mixture into ½ to ¾ inch balls

4. Place on pan and flatten into cookie shape

5. Place pan into the oven and cook for approximately 9-11 minutes

6. Remove cookies from oven and cool

Edible Hands (from refrigerated cookie dough)

Ingredients (cookies):

- Refrigerated sugar cookie dough

- All purpose flour (optional)

- Your choice of frosting and candies/ sprinkles to decorate

Directions:

1. Remove desired amount of dough from the wrapper

2. Grease Pans

3. Flatten cookie dough and cover the entire bottom of pan with it.

4. Place hand on top of cookie dough and press down to make a handprint

5. Carefully trim away excess dough from around handprint using a knife (Adult assistance required for this one)

6. Place pan and cookie into freezer for 15 minutes

7. Preheat Oven

8. Remove handprint from freezer and place in oven

9. Cook approximately 6-9 minutes until edges are golden brown

10. Cool Completely

Decorate hand using frosting and candies. Get creative here. You can use different candies for form a bracelet or a ring. You can also make "fingernails" on your hand by placing the same colored candy on the tip of each finger

Peanut Butter Cookie Cups (from cookie dough)

Ingredients:

- 1 package refrigerated peanut butter cookie dough

- Hershey's kisses

Directions:

1. Preheat oven. Spray pans with nonstick spray

2. Roll cookie mixture into ½ to ¾ inch balls

3. Place on pan and flatten into cookie shape

4. Place pan into the oven and cook for approximately 9-11 minutes

5. Unwrap 1 Hershey's kiss for each cookie

6. Remove cookies from oven

7. Place one Hershey's kiss on top of each cookie and press down into cookie as the chocolate begins to melt

Cake Batter Peanut Butter Cookies (from box mix)

Ingredients:

- 4 tablespoons yellow cake mix

- 2 tablespoon egg (beaten) or applesauce

- ½ tablespoon brown sugar

- 2 tablespoons peanut butter

- 1 teaspoon water

- ½ tablespoon oil

Topping:

- Sugar

Directions:

1. Preheat oven. Spray pans with nonstick spray

2. Mix ingredients together in small bowl

3. Roll cookie mixture into 1 inch balls

4. Roll cookies in granulated sugar to coat

5. Place on pan and flatten into cookie shape

6. Place pan into the oven and cook for approximately 9 minutes

7. Remove cookies from oven and cool

Cookie Pops (from refrigerated cookie dough)

Ingredients (cookies):

- Refrigerated cookie dough- any flavor (1/8 of roll)

- All purpose flour (optional)

- Your choice of frosting and candies/ sprinkles to decorate

Also Needed:

- 4 inch lollipop sticks (can usually be found in most big box retailers bakery section or arts & crafts stores)

- Small cookie cutters

Directions:

1. Preheat oven and spray pans with nonstick spray

2. Remove about 1/8 of the dough from the wrapper

3. Roll dough on floured surface to about ¼ inch thick

4. Cut out cookies with small cookie cutters. Place one cookie on the pan near the end (leave enough room for it to expand though).

5. Lay lollipop stick so that end of stick in on top of cookie at least ½ inch. Press down slightly so that lollipop tip is embedded in the cookie

6. Gently turn cookie over so that the stick in now on the bottom

7. Bake until edges are slightly brown (7-9 minutes)

8. Decorate with frosting, candies, etc…

Chocolate Cookies (from mug mix)

Ingredients:

- 1 Packet Chocolate Cake Mug Mix

- 1 tablespoon milk

Directions:

1. Preheat oven. Spray pans with nonstick spray

2. Mix ingredients together in small bowl

3. Roll cookie mixture into ½ to ¾ inch balls

4. Place on pan and flatten into cookie shape

5. Place pan into the oven and cook for approximately 9-11 minutes

6. Remove cookies from oven and cool

Yummy Cookie Butter Cookies (from scratch)

Ingredients:

- 3 tablespoons all purpose flour

- 1 tablespoon egg (beaten) or applesauce

- 1 tablespoon brown sugar

- 1 tablespoon butter (melted)

- 1 tablespoons semi- sweet chocolate chips

- 1 tablespoon Nutella™

Directions:

1. Preheat oven. Spray pans with nonstick spray

2. Mix ingredients together in small bowl

3. Drop mixture by spoonful onto pan

4. Place pan into the oven and cook for approximately 9-11 minutes

5. Remove cookies from oven and cool

Chocolate Peanut Butter Sandwich Cookies

Ingredients (cookies):

- 4 tablespoons yellow cake mix

- 2 tablespoon egg (beaten) or applesauce

- ½ tablespoon brown sugar

- 2 tablespoons peanut butter

- 1 teaspoon water

- ½ tablespoon oil

Topping:

- Sugar

- Chocolate frosting

Directions:

1. Preheat oven. Spray pans with nonstick spray

2. Mix cookie ingredients together in small bowl

3. Roll cookie mixture into 1 inch balls

4. Roll cookies in granulated sugar to coat

5. Place on pan and flatten into cookie shape

6. Place pan into the oven and cook for approximately 8-10 minutes

7. Remove cookies from oven and cool

8. Spread chocolate frosting of choice on bottom of two cookies and press together to form the chocolate peanut butter sandwich

Lady Finger Cookies (from scratch)

Ingredients:

- 4 tablespoons all purpose flour

- 1 tablespoon powdered sugar

- 2 tablespoons butter (softened)

- 1/8 teaspoon vanilla extract

- 2 tablespoons chopped pecans or walnuts

- Additional powdered sugar to roll warm cookies in

Directions:

1. Preheat oven. Spray pans with nonstick spray

2. Mix cookie ingredients together in small bowl

3. Roll cookie mixture into desired shape

4. Roll cookie in additional powdered sugar

5. Place on pan and flatten into cookie shape

6. Place pan into the oven and cook for approximately 9-11 minutes

7. Remove cookies from oven and immediately roll in powdered sugar again to coat the cookies

Chocolate Peanut Butter Cookies (from box mix)

Ingredients:

- 4 tablespoons chocolate fudge cake mix

- 1 ½ tablespoon eggs (beaten) or applesauce

- 1/8 teaspoon vanilla extract

- 1 ½ tablespoons peanut butter

- 3 tablespoons semi- sweet chocolate chips

- ½ tablespoon water

Directions:

1. Preheat oven. Spray pans with nonstick spray

2. Mix ingredients together in small bowl

3. Roll cookie mixture into ½ to ¾ inch balls

4. Place on pan and flatten into cookie shape

5. Place pan into the oven and cook for approximately 9-11 minutes

6. Remove cookies from oven and cool

7. Frost with icing of choice or thawed whipped topping if desired

Strawberry Cups (from refrigerated cookie dough)

Ingredients (cookies):

- Refrigerated sugar cookie dough

- All purpose flour (optional)

- 2 tablespoons strawberry preserves (*can choose a different flavor preserves if you prefer)

Directions:

1. Remove about 2-3 ounces of dough from the wrapper

2. Roll dough into ¾ inch balls

3. Using your thumb, press down in the center of each ball to form a deep indention making it look like a small "mini" bowl. Flatten slightly to fit in pan

4. Place cookies in freezer for 20 minutes

5. Preheat oven and spray pans with nonstick spray

6. Bake until edges are just slightly brown (usually 8-10 minutes

7. Remove from oven and press back down in center of cookie with the tip of a spoon to form your "mini" bowl again.

8. Place cookies back in oven and cook for an additional 2-3 minutes. Cookies should be golden brown

9. Remove from oven and cool cookies completely

10. Fill the center of your cookie with strawberry preserves

Chocolate Peanut Butter Cups (cookie dough)

Ingredients (cookies):

•   Refrigerated chocolate cookie dough

•   All purpose flour (optional)

•   2 tablespoons peanut butter frosting (recipe in frosting section)

Directions:

1. Remove about 2-3 ounces of dough from the wrapper

2. Roll dough into ¾ inch balls

3. Using your thumb, press down in the center of each ball to form a deep indention making it look like a small "mini" bowl

4. Place cookies in freezer for 20 minutes

5. Preheat oven and spray pans with nonstick spray

6. Bake until edges are just slightly browned (usually 8-10 minutes

7. Remove from oven and press back down in center of cookie with the tip of a spoon to form your "mini" bowl again.

8. Place cookies back in oven and cook for an additional 2-3 minutes. Cookies should be firm and set

9. Remove from oven and cool cookies completely

10. Fill center of your cookie "bowl" with peanut butter frosting

Basic Sandwich Cookies (from refrigerated dough)

Ingredients (cookies):

- Any flavor refrigerated cookie dough

- All purpose flour (optional)

Filling:

- Your choice of assorted frostings, ice cream or peanut butter

- Sprinkles or assorted candies (ex. M&M's ™)

Directions:

1. Preheat oven. Spray pans with nonstick spray

2. Remove desired amount of cookie dough from wrapper (depending on how many cookies you want to make). Refrigerate remaining dough

3. Roll dough to ¼ inch thickness. You can sprinkle a little flour down first to keep the cookies from sticking if you'd like.

4. Cut out cookies using a small round cookie cutter

5. Place cookies on sheet making sure to leave enough room between them (1-2 inches)

6. Bake until edges are just slightly brown (usually 8-10 minutes)

7. Remove and allow cookies to cool completely

8. Spread desired filling on the underside of the 1st cookie. Top with the second cookie and press together

9. Roll cookie edges in sprinkles or assorted candies

Birthday Cake Cookies (from box mix)

Ingredients:

- 4 tablespoons funfetti cake mix

- 1 tablespoon egg (beaten) or applesauce

- ½ teaspoon vanilla extract

- ½ tablespoon butter (softened)

- 1/8 teaspoon baking powder

- 1/8 teaspoon vanilla extract

- 2 tablespoons sprinkles

Directions:

1. Preheat oven. Spray pans with nonstick spray

2. Mix ingredients together in small bowl

3. Roll cookie mixture into 1 inch balls

4. Place on pan and flatten into cookie shape

5. Place pan into the oven and cook for approximately 9-11 minutes

6. Remove cookies from oven and cool

7. Top with frosting & sprinkles for that true birthday cake feel

Chapter 3: Glazings and Frostings Recipes

Crystal Sugar Frosting

Ingredients:

- 4 teaspoons vegetable shortening

- 2/3 cup powdered sugar

- 1/4 teaspoon vanilla

- 1 teaspoon milk

- Colored sugar crystals; optional

Directions:

1. Mix together all ingredients until smooth and creamy.

2. Sprinkle with colored sugar crystals, if desired.

Lemon Frosting

Ingredients:

- 1/4 cup powdered sugar

- 1 teaspoon lemon juice

- 1 teaspoon water

Directions:

1. Mix sugar, lemon juice and water together.

2. Stir until smooth.

3. Add water to thin if required.

4. Add more powdered sugar to thicken if necessary.

Makes frosting for 1 - 2 single layer cakes

Strawberry Frosting

Ingredients:

- 1/4 cup confectioners' sugar

- 1 teaspoon strawberry drink powder

- 2 teaspoons water

Directions:

1. Combine confectioners' sugar and drink powder.

2. Add 2 teaspoons water and stir until smooth.

3. If frosting is too thick, add a little water.

4. If frosting is too thin, add a little powdered sugar.

Makes enough to frost two layers of cake

Garlic Glaze

Ingredients:

- 1 tablespoon butter

- 1/8 teaspoon garlic powder

- 1/4 teaspoon dried parsley

Directions:

1. Melt the butter in a warming tray.

2. Stir the garlic powder and parsley flakes into the melted butter.

3. Brush the mixture over warm biscuits (such as cheese biscuits).

Cream Cheese Frosting

Make-Ahead Mix

(Divide ingredients by 8 to make an individual frosting)

Ingredients:

- 2 cup confectioners' sugar

- 4 1/2 teaspoons instant nonfat milk powder

- 3 tablespoons cream cheese

Directions:

1. Combine sugar and powdered milk, blending with a wire whisk.

2. Cut in cream cheese.

3. Spoon 1/3 cup mixture into each of 8 containers or re-sealable bags.

4. Seal tightly and label with date and contents.

5. Store in refrigerator for up to 2 weeks.

To use frosting:

1. Add 3/4 teaspoon water to 1 package cream cheese frosting mix.

2. Add a drop of almond extract.

3. Combine well with spoon until smooth and creamy.

Makes 1/4 cup of frosting - enough to frost a double layer cake

Great for carrot cake, pumpkin cake or spice cakes

Peppermint Frosting

Ingredients:

- 1/4 cup confectioners' sugar

- 1/2 cup butter

- 1/2 teaspoon peppermint extract

Directions:

1. Mix sugar, butter and extract until smooth.

2. Spread evenly over cooled brownies or cookies.

3. Chill until set.

Vanilla Frosting #1

Ingredients:

-   1/4 c. confectioners' sugar

-   2 drops vanilla

-   1 teaspoon water

Directions:

1. Combine all 3 ingredients.

2. Mix until it reaches a smooth, desired consistency.

Vanilla Frosting #2

Ingredients:

-   4 teaspoons butter

-   2/3 cup powdered sugar

-   1/4 teaspoon vanilla

-   2 teaspoons milk

Directions:

1. In a small bowl, mix all ingredients together until smooth and creamy.

2. Spread 2 teaspoons of frosting on top of 1st layer of cake.

3. Add 2nd layer and continue frosting.

Buttercream Frosting

Make-Ahead Mix

(Divide ingredients by 8 to make an individual frosting)

Ingredients:

- 2 cups confectioners' sugar

- 3 tablespoons instant non-fat milk powder

- 6 tablespoons butter

Directions:

1. Combine confectioners' sugar and powdered milk, mix well.

2. Cut in butter with pastry blender.

3. Spoon about 1/3 cup mixture into each of 8 small containers or re-sealable bags.

4. Seal tightly and label with date and contents.

5. Store in refrigerator.

6. Use within 12 weeks.

Makes about 8 packages frosting

To use frosting:

1. Add 3/4 teaspoon water to 1 package butter cream frosting mix.

2. In a small bowl, combine the mix and water.

3. Stir well with a spoon until smooth and creamy.

Peanut Butter Frosting

Make-Ahead Mix

(Divide ingredients by 8 to make an individual frosting)

Ingredients:

- 2 cups confectioners' sugar

- 3 tablespoons instant non-fat milk powder

- 6 tablespoons peanut butter

Directions:

1. Combine confectioners' sugar and powdered milk, mix well.

2. Cut in peanut butter with pastry blender.

3. Spoon about 1/3 cup mixture into each 8 small containers or re-sealable bags.

4. Seal tightly and label with date and contents.

5. Store in refrigerator.

6. Use within 12 weeks.

Makes 8 Packages

To use frosting:

1. Add 3/4 teaspoon water to 1 package Butter Cream Frosting mix in a small bowl.

2. Add a drop or two of vanilla if desired.

3. Stir well with a spoon until smooth and creamy.

Makes about 1/4 cup of frosting

Watermelon Frosting

Make-Ahead Mix

(Divide ingredients by 8 to make an individual frosting)

Ingredients:

- 2 cups confectioners' sugar

- 3 tablespoon instant non-fat milk powder

- 1 teaspoon watermelon drink powder

- 6 tablespoons butter

Directions:

1. In a medium size bowl, combine sugar, milk powder and drink powder, stirring well.

2. Cut butter into mix.

3. Measure about 1/3 cup in each of 8 containers or re-sealable bags.

4. Store in refrigerator up to three months.

Makes 8 packages of watermelon frosting

To use frosting:

1. Add 3/4 teaspoon water to one package mix in a small bowl.

2. Mix until smooth.

Orange Glaze

Ingredients:

1. 1 tablespoon fresh squeezed orange juice

2. 1 tablespoon sugar

3. 1/2 teaspoon orange zest

Directions:

1. Mix all the ingredients together.

White Frosting

Make-Ahead Mix

(Divide ingredients by 8 to make an individual frosting)

Ingredients:

- 2 cups sifted confectioners' sugar

- 3 tablespoons instant nonfat milk powder

- 6 tablespoons butter

Directions:

1. Combine all ingredients, blending well.

2. Spoon about 1/3 cup of mixture into each of 8 small containers or re-sealable bags.

3. Seal bags tightly and label with date and contents.

4. Store in refrigerator.

5. Use within 12 weeks.

Makes 8 packages white frosting mix.

To use frosting:

1. Mix 3/4 teaspoon water with 1 package frosting in a small bowl.

2. Add a drop or two of vanilla if desired.

3. Stir well with a spoon until smooth and creamy.

Makes about 1/4 cup frosting

Chocolate Frosting

Make-Ahead Mix

(Divide ingredients by 8 to make an individual frosting)

Ingredients:

- 2 cups confectioners' sugar

- 3 tablespoons instant nonfat milk powder

- 1/2 cup unsweetened cocoa powder

- 6 tablespoons butter

Directions:

1. Combine all ingredients until mixture resembles crumbs.

2. Spoon about 1/3 cup of mixture into each of 8 small containers or re-sealable bags.

3. Seal tightly and label with date and contents.

4. Store in refrigerator.

5. Use within 12 weeks.

Makes 8 packages of Frosting

To use frosting:

1. Add 3/4 tsp. water to 1 pkg. chocolate frosting mix in a small bowl.

2. Combine well and stir with a spoon until smooth.

Makes about 1/4 cup

Sparkling Frosting

Ingredients:

- 4 teaspoons butter

- 2/3 cup confectioners' sugar

- 1/4 teaspoon vanilla

- 2 teaspoons milk

- Colored sugar crystals for decoration

Directions:

1. In a small bowl, mix together butter, confectioners' sugar, vanilla and milk until smooth and creamy.

2. Spread 2 teaspoons of frosting on top of 1st layer of cake.

3. Add 2nd layer and continue frosting.

4. Sprinkle with colored crystal sugars.

Frosts a 2 layer cake

Chapter 4: Main Course Baking Recipes

Lasagna

This recipe needs the following ingredients:

★ A single pound of beef that is ground and lean

★ 32 ounces of cottage cheese

★ A single jar of spaghetti sauce (32 ounces)

★ 2 eggs

★ 2 teaspoons of parsley (dried)

★ Half a cup of grated parmesan cheese

★ 3 cups of mozzarella cheese that is shredded

★ 9 lasagna noodles

★ Half a cup of water

The steps you need to complete this dish are the following:

1. Get a large skillet.

2. Put your heat to medium.

3. Brown your ground beef before draining all the grease.

4. Add the sauce and simmer for 5 minutes.

5. Get a bowl.

6. Mix mozzarella cheese (leave one cup out), eggs, cottage cheese, spices, and half of the parmesan cheese.

7. Get a baking dish that is 9 by 13.

8. Spread ¾ of the sauce mix in the pan and then place 3 lasagna noodles (uncooked) over it.

9. Then place the remaining mozzarella and parmesan cheese.

10. Add half a cup of water to your edges of the pan.

11. Cover with your aluminum foil.

12. Heat your oven to 350 F.

13. Bake for 45 minutes.

14. Uncover your dish.

15. Bake ten more minutes.

16. Let it stand for ten minutes; then it's ready.

This recipe will take an hour and a half to complete.

Nutritional information (per serving):

➢ Calories-377

➢ Fat-26.4 grams

➢ Carbs-26.4 grams

➢ Protein-29.4 grams

Chicken Pot Pie

Chicken pot pie is a classic, and it's been around forever. Many find it comforting and make it people happy when they eat it.

The ingredients that you will need for this dish are as follows:

★ A single teaspoon of thyme (dried)

★ A single cup of cubed butter

★ 2 cups of potatoes that are peeled and diced

★ ⅔ of a cup of onion that is chopped

★ A single cup of peas that are frozen

★ A cup of corn that is frozen

★ 3 cups of chicken broth

★ A single cup of all-purpose flour

★ A single cup and ¾ of carrots that are sliced

★ 4 sheets of pie crust (refrigerated)

★ ¾ teaspoon of pepper

★ A single teaspoon and ¾ of salt

★ A single cup and a half of whole milk

★ 4 cups of chicken (cooked and cubed)

The steps you will need for this dish are as follows:

1. Make sure that your oven is preheated to 425.

2. Place your carrots and potatoes in a saucepan.

3. You will need to add water to cover.

4. Bring it to a boil.

5. Reduce your heat and then cover and cook for 10 minutes.

6. They should be tender and crispy.

7. Drain.

8. Get a large skillet.

9. Heat your butter over a heat that is medium-high.

10. Add in the onion and cook it until it's tender. Don't forget to stir.

11. Stir in the seasonings and the flour until it has blended.

12. Slowly stir in your milk and broth before bringing it to a boil. Stir constantly here.

13. Cook and stir it for an additional 2 minutes.

14. It should be thickened now.

15. Stir in your potato, corn, chicken, and peas mix and remove from the heat.

16. Unroll your pie crust into a 9-inch pie plate. Trim, so it's even with the rim of the plate.

17. Add in the chicken mix.

18. Unroll the other crusts and place over your filling.

19. Trim it and seal it.

20. Flute the edges.

21. Cut slits in the tops.

22. Bake for 40 minutes, and you should see a crust that is lightly browned.

23. Let it stand for a quarter of an hour before you cut it.

This recipe will make 2 pot pies at eight servings each.

You will need an hour and 15 minutes to complete this dish.

Nutritional information (per serving):

➢ Calories-475

➢ Fat-28 grams

➢ Carbs-41 grams

➢ Protein-15 grams

➢ Fiber- 2 grams

Baked Ziti

Savory and very filling this are another dish that is a good start for becoming a great chef.

The ingredients you will need for this recipe is as follows:

★ A single onion that has been chopped

★ 2 jars of spaghetti sauce (26-ounce jars)

★ A single pound of ziti pasta (dry)

★ A single pound of ground beef that is lean

★ A single cup and a half of sour cream

★ 2 tablespoons of parmesan cheese that is grated

★ 6 ounces of provolone cheese that has been sliced

★ 6 ounces of mozzarella cheese that has been shredded

The steps to complete this dish are as follows:

1. Get a large pot.

2. Bring a pot of water that has been lightly salted to a boil.

3. Add pasta and cook till al dente. This is for approximately 8 minutes.

4. Drain it.

5. Get a skillet.

6. In the skillet brown the beef and onion over a heat of medium.

7. Add the sauce and simmer for a quarter of an hour.

8. Preheat your oven to 350.

9. Get a baking dish that is 9 by 13.

10. Butter the baking dish.

11. Layer the dish with half of the ziti, provolone cheese, sour cream, half of the sauce mix, the remaining ziti and then the mozzarella and the rest of the sauce.

12. Top with the parmesan.

13. Bake a half-hour, and the cheese should be melted.

This recipe will take you an hour to complete.

Nutritional information (per serving):

➢ Calories-578

➢ Fat-25.3 grams

➢ Carbs-58.4 grams

➢ Protein-27.9 grams

Chicken Fiesta Bake

The ingredients for this recipe are as follows:

★ 2-3 chicken breasts that have been sliced widthwise in half

★ Taco seasoning

★ Half a cup of medium cheddar cheese

★ Diced green onion

★ A single 16 ounce of salsa (medium)

★ A single can of undrained corn

★ A cup of rice that is white and long grain

★ A third of a cup of water

★ A single can of drained and rinsed black beans

The steps to complete this recipe are as follows:

1. Get a pan that is 9 by 13 and grease it with cooking spray.

2. Place everything in the pan except the chicken and seasoning.

3. Place the chicken on top of the rest of the ingredients and place seasoning on top of the chicken.

4. Bake at 375 for 45 minutes.

5. Place the cheese on the top and bake for 5 minutes more.

6. Top with green onions.

This recipe will give you four servings.

This recipe will take you an hour to complete.

Pizza

The ingredients that you will need for this recipe is as follows:

★ A single pound and a half of pizza dough

★ A single cup of basil leaves that are torn and fresh

★ 8 ounces of sliced mozzarella cheese

★ 28 ounce can of tomatoes that are whole, peeled and drained

★ 4 large minced garlic cloves

The steps needed for this dish are the following:

1. Heat your oven to 450 degrees.

2. If you choose to use a pizza stone in the oven to warm.

3. Roll out your dough on a surface that is lightly floured.

4.   Press into a large circle gently and make sure that it is a quarter-inch thick.

For the sauce:

1.   Get a bowl.

2.   Crush the tomatoes in the bowl.

3.   Add garlic and spices (salt and pepper) in the bowl and stir it before placing it to the side.

4.   Place the sauce on the dough and then add cheese and half of the basil.

Last instructions:

1.   Bake for 25 minutes until the cheese is bubbling and the crust is golden in color. Place the rest of the basil on top.

Nutritional information (per serving, 2 slices):

➢ Calories-390

➢ Fat-11 grams

➢ Carbs- 52 grams

➢ Protein-15 grams

➢ Fiber- 3 grams

Shepherd's Pie

The ingredients that you will need for this recipe is as follows:

★ A single tablespoon of butter

★ A single tablespoon of onion that has been chopped finely

★ 4 potatoes that are cubed, peeled and large in size

★ A quarter cup of cheddar cheese that has been shredded

★ 5 chopped carrots

★ A single chopped onion

★ A single pound of ground beef that is lean

★ 2 tablespoons of flour (use all-purpose)

★ A single tablespoon of vegetable oil

★ A single tablespoon of ketchup

★ A quarter cup of cheddar cheese that is shredded

★ ¾ of a cup of broth that is beef

The steps needed for this dish are as follows:

1. Get a large pot and add salted water to it before bringing it to a boil.

2. Add your potatoes and cook them until they are firm but tender. This should take a quarter of an hour.

3. Drain it before mashing it.

4. Mix in your butter and the onion that is finely chopped along with a quarter cup of the cheese that is shredded.

5. Season and place to the side.

6. Bring a large pot of water that has been salted to a boil and add your carrots. Cook them for a quarter of an hour until firm but tender.

7. Drain and mash them before setting aside.

8. Heat your oven to 375 F.

9. Heat your oil in a frying pan.

10. Add your onion and cook it until it's clear.

11. Add beef and cook until it has been browned well.

12. Pour off that excess fat and stir in your flour.

13. Cook for 60 seconds.

14. Add your ketchup and then your broth.

15. Bring to a boil and then reduce your heat and simmer for 5 minutes.

16. Get a casserole dish (2 quarts).

17. Spread the beef in a layer before adding the carrots and potatoes.

18. Place your cheese on top.

19. Bake for 20 minutes. It should have a golden brown color.

This recipe will take an hour to complete.

Nutritional information (per serving):

➢ Calories-452

➢ Fat-17 grams

➢ Carbs-52.5 grams

Roasted Whole Chicken with Root Vegetables

Nutritious and delicious. This is a great dish for any chef to learn and become familiar with.

The ingredients you will need for this recipe are as follows:

★ A whole chicken (four pounds)

★ 2 tablespoons of fresh rosemary (you need it to be finely chopped and an additional three sprigs for the cavity)

★ A single tablespoon of fresh sage (chopped and four additional sprigs for the cavity)

★ A single teaspoon and a half of red pepper flakes

★ 6 tablespoons of olive oil

★ 2 tablespoons of fresh thyme (chopped finely and 3 additional sprigs for the cavity)

★ 4 carrots (slender and peeled)

★ The zest of a single lemon and a half of a lemon

★ 2 garlic cloves that are grated finely (you need the remaining head of garlic, and you will need to halve it in a horizontal manner to expose the cloves in each half)

★ 2 bay leaves

★ A single turnip that is medium in size (you need to peel it and cut it into ¾ inch pieces)

★ A single pound of rutabaga (peel it and cut it into ¾ inch pieces. Cubes will look aesthetically pleasing. Don't eat or use the leaves at all)

The steps you will need to complete this dish are as follows:

1. Make sure your oven is preheated to 375 F.

2. Place your chicken on a baking pan that is rimmed.

3. Get a small bowl.

4. Place the pepper flakes, garlic, zest, rosemary, sage, thyme, oil, a single teaspoon of salt, and two of the pepper in the bowl. Stir everything to make sure that it is combining.

5. Rub your chicken completely with half of the herb oil. Make sure that you get some under the skin of the thighs and breasts.

6. Stuff the cavity with your sprigs of thyme, rosemary, and sage, along with your bay leaves, half lemon and garlic head halves that you made.

7. Place your veggies in a bowl.

8. Toss the veggies in the remaining oil mixture.

9. Place the veggies around the chicken and put it in the oven.

10. Roast until the vegetables have become tender, and the chicken has been cooked through. You will be able to tell it's done with a thermometer that is instant-read and insert it into the thickest part of the thigh. It should read 160 degrees F at around the time of an hour and 15 minutes.

11. Let it sit for 10 minutes before you carve it.

This recipe will give you 8 servings.

You will need 2 and a half hours to complete this dish.

Nutritional Information (per serving):

➢ Calories-564

➢ Fiber-3 grams

➢ Fat-35 grams

➢ Protein-51 grams

➢ Carbs-12 grams

Meatloaf

The ingredients that you need are as follows:

★ Half a teaspoon of both salt and pepper (ground pepper)

★ Half a cup of diced onion

★ A single egg

★ A single cup of grated parmesan cheese

★ 16 ounces of ground beef that is 90% grass-fed and lean

★ A quarter of a cup of ketchup and a third of a cup of ketchup

The steps for the recipe that you will need to do are the following:

1.   Heat the oven to 350 F.

2.   Get a loaf pan.

3.   Line it with aluminum foil.

4.   Dice the onion finely.

5.   Mix all of your ingredients in a bowl except for the last third of a cup of ketchup. Either use your hands or something to stir it.

6.   Form it into a loaf and stick it in the pan topping it with the rest of the ketchup.

7.   Bake for 60 minutes.

8.   When finished, let stand for 5 minutes.

This recipe will give you 4 servings.

This recipe will take you an hour and 10 minutes to complete.

Nutritional information (per serving):

➢ Calories-342

➢ Fat-17.5 grams

➢ Protein-36.2 grams

➢ Carbs-9.6 grams

Chicken & Rice Casserole

The ingredients for this recipe are as follows:

★ 4 breasts of chicken

★ A cup and a half of water

★ A single of white rice that is uncooked and long grain

★ A single package of onion soup mix

★ A single 10 ounce can of cream of mushroom soup that is condensed

The steps to complete this recipe are as follows:

1. Heat your oven to 325 F.

2. Get a 9 by 13 pan and spray it with cooking spray.

3. Add your chicken and season it (with pepper and salt)

4. Pour the rice over the chicken. The rice should be uncooked.

5. Sprinkle with the soup mix.

6. Combine the water and the soup and pour it over the chicken.

7. Cover it and then bake it for an hour and fifteen minutes. The rice should be tender.

This recipe will give you 4 servings.

This recipe will take you an hour and a half to complete.

Nutritional information (per serving):

➢ Calories-470

➢ Fat- 7 grams

➢ Carbs- 40 grams

➢ Protein- 54 grams

Baked Macaroni and Cheese

The ingredients that you will need for this recipe are as follows:

★ A quarter of a teaspoon of mustard (ground)

★ A single tablespoon and a half of butter that has been cut into small pieces

★ 2 cups of milk that is low fat

★ A single pound of sharp shredded cheddar cheese

★ A single package of elbow macaroni

★ 2 tablespoons of flour that is all-purpose

★ A quarter teaspoon of salt

★ A quarter of a teaspoon of black pepper

The steps that you will need to complete for this recipe are the following:

1. Have an oven that is preheated to 375 F.

2. Get a 9 by 13 casserole dish.

3. Stay the dish.

4. Cook the macaroni, when it's tender, drain it.

5. When the pasta is cooking, combine the 2 and a half cups of cheese with the mustard, flour, and pepper.

6. Get a bowl and combine the cheese mix you just made with the hot pasta and stir it to combine.

7. Pour into the pan.

8. Pour your milk over the pasta.

9. Top the dish with cheese.

10. Dot with butter.

11. Cover with aluminum foil.

12. Bake for 45 minutes. If you choose to, you can take the foil off at the half-hour mark.

13. It should be firm and a brownish golden color.

14. If you let it sit for 10 minutes before serving, you should be able to let it firm up further.

This recipe will give you six servings.

You will need 90 minutes for this recipe.

Nutritional information (per serving):

➢ Calories-220

➢ Fat- 6 grams

➢ Carbs-34 grams

➢ Protein-10 grams

➢ Fiber-5 grams

Chapter 5: Bars Recipes

Raspberry Bars

Note:

To make Strawberry Bars, substitute the raspberry jam for strawberry jam.

Ingredients:

- 3 tablespoons flour
- 1 tablespoon crushed cornflakes
- 1 tablespoon soft butter
- 1 teaspoon sugar
- 2 teaspoons raspberry jam

Directions:

1. Mix together flour, cornflakes, butter and sugar in a bowl until crumbly.
2. Reserve 2 tablespoons of mixture.
3. Press remaining mixture firmly into oven pan.
4. Spread with jam.
5. Sprinkle reserved mixture over jam.
6. Press down gently.
7. Bake for 18 minutes.
8. Remove from oven to cool.
9. Cut into bars.

Oatmeal Fruit Bars

Ingredients:

- 1 tablespoon soft butter

- 6 teaspoons brown sugar

- Dash salt

- 1/4 cup flour

- 1/8 teaspoon baking soda

- 2 tablespoons quick cooking rolled oats

- 3 tablespoons milk

- 2 teaspoons apple sauce or marmalade

Directions:

1. Mix butter, sugar and salt until creamed.

2. Add flour, baking soda, oats, and milk.

3. Mix well until it forms soft dough.

4. Place 1/2 of the mixture in a greased pan.

5. Press down in pan with fingertips or back of spoon.

6. Spread with 2 teaspoons apple sauce or marmalade

7. Bake about 20 minutes.

8. Let cool and cut into bars.

Recipe makes 2 pans

Granola Bars

Ingredients:

- 1/4 cup rolled oats

- 3 teaspoons all-purpose flour

- 1/8 teaspoon baking soda

- 1/8 teaspoon vanilla extract

- 2 teaspoons softened butter

- 1 teaspoon honey

- 1 teaspoon packed brown sugar

- 1 teaspoon semisweet mini chocolate chips

- 1 teaspoon raisins

Directions:

1. Combine oats, flour, soda, vanilla, butter, honey and sugar.

2. Add in chocolate chips and raisins.

3. Lightly press the mixture into a greased and floured oven pan.

4. Bake for 10 minutes.

5. Let cool for 10 minutes.

6. Cut into bars.

Apple Bar

Ingredients:

- 3 tablespoons flour

- 1 tablespoon crushed cornflakes (or other similar cereal)

- 1 tablespoon soft butter

- 1 teaspoon sugar

- 2 teaspoons apple jelly

- 1/8 teaspoon cinnamon; optional

Directions:

1. In a bowl, mix flour, cinnamon, cereal, butter and sugar until crumbly.

2. Reserve 2 tablespoons of the crumbly mixture.

3. Press remaining mixture firmly into pan.

4. Spread with jelly.

5. Sprinkle reserved crumbly mixture over jelly.

6. Press gently with fingers.

7. Bake for 18 minutes.

8. Cool.

9. Cut into slices.

6-Layer Bar

Ingredients:

- 2 tablespoons butter

- 1/3 cup graham wafer crumbs

- 2 tablespoons semisweet chocolate chips

- 2 tablespoons butterscotch chips

- 2 tablespoons flaked coconut

- 2 tablespoons chopped walnuts

- 2 tablespoons sweetened condensed milk

Directions:

1. Melt butter in an oven baking pan.

2. Remove from oven.

3. Sprinkle graham cracker crumbs evenly over butter.

4. Layer chocolate and butterscotch chips.

5. Add a layer of flaked coconut.

6. Sprinkle walnuts on top.

7. Pour condensed milk evenly over everything.

8. Bake about 15 minutes.

Chocolate Peanut Butter Bars

Ingredients:

- Peanut butter

- Graham crackers

- Mini chocolate chips

Directions:

1. Spread a thin layer of peanut butter on a graham cracker.

2. Top with mini chocolate chips.

3. Bake for 5 minutes to melt the chocolate chips.

4. Remove and spread the softened chocolate chips.

5. Allow bar to cool slightly before eating.

Chapter 6: Brownies Recipes

Notes:

1. Remember that brownies do not look the same as a cake during baking.

2. Brownie baking time may vary, depending on the model of your oven.

3. Older ovens cook at approximate 375F and will take about 12 minutes.

4. Newer ovens tend to cook at around 350F so they'll take approximately 14-16 minutes.

5. Do not cook longer than 17 minutes.

Brownies Mix #1

Ingredients:

- 2-1/2 tablespoons flour

- 2 teaspoons sugar

- 1 teaspoon coconut oil (or olive oil)

- Pinch baking soda

- Dash salt

- 1 teaspoon baking cocoa

- 1/8 teaspoon vanilla extract

- 4 teaspoons milk

- 2 teaspoons chocolate syrup

Directions:

1. In a small bowl combine all of the ingredients.

2. Mix well until smooth.

3. Pour batter into greased and floured cake pan.

4. Bake 12-15 minutes or according to your oven directions.

5. Remove from oven and cool before cutting.

Brownies Mix #2

Ingredients:

- 2 tablespoons sugar
- 2-1/2 tablespoons flour
- 1 teaspoon oil
- 1/8 teaspoon baking powder
- 1/8 teaspoon vanilla extract
- 2 teaspoons chocolate syrup
- 2 teaspoons milk
- 1 teaspoon baking cocoa

Directions:

1. Blend all ingredients until the batter is smooth.
2. Pour batter into greased and floured cake pan.
3. Bake 14-17 minutes or until done.

Mint Chocolate Brownies

Ingredients:

- 2 tablespoons white sugar
- 1 tablespoon softened butter
- 3 tablespoons chocolate syrup
- 2 tablespoons all-purpose flour

Directions:

1. Grease a baking dish.
2. Cream together sugar and butter until smooth.
3. Stir in chocolate syrup.

4. Stir in flour until blended.

5. Spread batter evenly into prepared pan.

6. Bake in oven for about 15 minutes.

7. Cool completely in pan.

8. Top with Peppermint Frosting

Graham Brownie Mix

Ingredients:

*   2-1/2 tablespoons flour

*   2 teaspoons sugar

*   1 teaspoon coconut oil

*   Pinch baking soda

*   Dash salt

*   1 teaspoon baking cocoa

*   1/8 teaspoon vanilla extract

*   4 teaspoons milk

*   2 teaspoons chocolate syrup

*   1/3 cup graham wafer crumbs

*   1 teaspoon cocoa

*   2 tablespoons chopped nuts

*   1 tablespoon sweetened condensed milk

Directions:

1. Blend all ingredients thoroughly.

2. Spread in well-buttered pan.

3. Bake 12-15 minutes or until done.

Double Fudge Brownies

Ingredients:

- 2 1/2 tablespoons sugar

- 1 teaspoon oil

- 1/8 teaspoon vanilla extract

- 4 teaspoons chocolate syrup

- 1/4 teaspoon baking coco

- 2 1/2 tablespoons flour

Directions:

1. Stir all ingredients together until the batter is smooth.

2. Pour the batter into a greased and floured pan.

3. Bake for 15 minutes.

4. Cool 5 minutes.

5. Cut & serve.

Chapter 7: Baked Snack Recipes

Banana Bread

The ingredients for this recipe are as follows:

★ A single teaspoon of baking soda

★ ¾ of a cup of sugar

★ Half a cup of pecans that have been chopped

★ 3 bananas medium in size and mashed

★ Half a cup of mayonnaise

★ A single egg

★ A cup and a half of flour

The steps to complete this recipe are as follows:

1.   Preheat your oven to 350.

2.   Get a bowl.

3.   Mix the egg, mayonnaise, and bananas.

4.   Get another bowl.

5.   Mix the baking soda, pecans, flour, and sugar in the bowl.

6.   Add the flour mix to the wet mix and stir until combined.

7.   The mix will be very thick; this is alright. If you over-mix, it won't be right.

8.   Grease a pan.

9.   Pour the mix into the pan and bake for an hour. A toothpick should come out clean.

10. Remove from the pan and make sure it cools completely.

This recipe will give you a dozen servings.

You will need an hour and ten minutes to complete this recipe.

Nutritional information (per serving):

➢ Calories-231

- ➤ Fat-10 grams

- ➤ Fiber- 1 gram

- ➤ Protein-2 grams

- ➤ Carbs-31 grams

Smoky Pretzel Mix

The ingredients for this recipe are as follows:

★ A single cup of almonds that are smoked

★ A single cup of mini pretzels

★ 2 teaspoons of chipotle chili powder

★ A single teaspoon of paprika that is smoked

★ 2 cups corn snack crackers

★ 2 cups of rice cereal squares

★ 2 cups of white cheddar cheese crackers in bite-size

★ 6 tablespoons of butter that is unsalted

The steps you need to complete are as follows:

1. Heat the oven to 325.

2. Toss everything together except the butter and spices in a bowl.

3. Melt the butter in a pan over medium heat.

4. Stir in chili powder, paprika, and garlic.

5. Drizzle over the mix.

6. Toss to coat evenly.

7. Spread it on a rimmed baking sheet that you lined with parchment paper.

8. Bake for 12 minutes. Stir once during this time.

9. Cool totally on the sheet.

10. Store in a container that is airtight.

This recipe will give you 10 servings.

This recipe will take a half-hour to complete.

Almond-Raisin Granola

The ingredients for this recipe are as follows:

★ Half a cup of flax seeds

★ Half a cup of sunflower seed kernels

★ A cup of raw almonds that are sliced

★ 3 cups of oats that are old-fashioned

★ A quarter cup of melted coconut oil

★ A single cup of raisins

★ 6 tablespoons of honey

★ 6 tablespoons of pure maple syrup

★ 2 tablespoons of water that is warm

The steps to complete this recipe are as follows:

1. Heat your oven to 250 and line a jelly roll pan with baking parchment.

2. Mix everything but the water, oil, honey, and syrup in a bowl and whisk the water, oil, honey, and syrup in another bowl. Make sure that the honey mix is smooth.

3. Pour the oat mix bowl into the honey bowl.

4. Spread the mix on the pan in a layer that is even.

5. Bake for an hour but up to an hour and a half until the color is a golden brown.

6. Take out of the oven and make sure that you let it cool completely.

7. Take the granola off by lifting the paper.

8. Break it and place in a bowl adding your choice of ingredients and then mix it.

9. Store in a container that is airtight.

This recipe will take you an hour and 45 minutes to complete.

Nutritional information (per serving):

➢ Calories-568

➢ Protein-12.4 grams

➢ Fat-27.2 grams

➢ Carbs0-76.4 grams

Lemon Raspberry Muffins

This recipe will require the following ingredients:

★ Half a cup of honey

★ 2 eggs

★ A single cup of plain Greek yogurt

★ A single cup and ¾ of white whole wheat flour

★ A single teaspoon of baking powder

★ Half a teaspoon of baking soda

★ A third of a cup of coconut oil that is melted

★ 2 teaspoons of vanilla extract

★ The zest from a lemon

★ A single cup and a half of organic raspberries

★ A single tablespoon of turbinado sugar

The steps that you will need to take to complete this recipe is the following:

1. Heat your oven to 350 F.

2. Grease a 12 cup muffin tin with coconut oil or cooking spray.

3. Get a large bowl.

4. Combine flour, baking soda, baking powder, and blend together with a whisk.

5. Get another bowl and combine the honey oil, and beat them together with a whisk.

6. Add in the eggs and beat them well before adding the zest, vanilla, and yogurt.

7. Mix it all well. If the oil gets solid, microwave it for half a minute.

8. Pour your wet ingredients into the dry.

9. Mix it with a large spoon until it has just combined.

10. Fold raspberries in the batter. It will be thick.

11. Divided into the 12 cups and add sugar to the top.

12. Bake 24 minutes and toothpick should come out clean.

13. Let cool on a cooling rack.

This recipe will give you 12 2 servings.

This recipe will take you an hour to finish.

Nutritional information (per serving):

➢ Calories-193

➢ Carbs-28.7 grams

➢ Fat-7.5 grams

➢ Protein-5.3 grams

Pizza Pockets

The ingredients for this recipe are as follows:

★ A third of a cup of Parmesan that is grated

★ A quarter of a cup of Parmesan that is grated

★ 8 ounces of turkey sausage (Italian)

★ A single tablespoon of olive oil

★ A single beaten egg

★ A single cup and a half of marinara sauce

★ All-purpose flour

★ A single pizza crust store-bought

★ 4 ounces of room temperature cream cheese

★ A cup of arugula tightly packed

The steps to complete this recipe are as follows:

1. Heat your olive oil over a heat that is medium-high and in a medium heavy skillet.

2. Add in the sausage and cook until it is golden and crumbled. 5 minutes.

3. Add the arugula and cook it until it has wilted.

4. Turn off your heat and let it cool for 19 minutes.

5. Add in your cream cheese and a third of the parmesan.

6. Stir, so it combines.

7. Set it aside.

8. Preheat your oven to 400 F.

9. Roll out your dough and make a big rectangle.

10. Cut it in half.

11. Do this again until you have eight equal rectangles.

12. Put your toppings onto one of the sides of each rectangle.

13. Brush the edges with egg wash.

14. Close the rectangle of dough over the topping.

15. Use a fork to seal them up.

16. Put the pockets on the baking sheet that is lined with parchment paper.

17. Brush the tops with egg wash.

18. Sprinkle the rest of the cheese on top.

19. Bake for 15 minutes.

20. Heat your marinara sauce over a low heat.

21. Serve with sauce when done.

This recipe will give you 4 servings

This recipe will take you 40 minutes to finish

Nutritional information (per serving):

➢ Calories-385

➢ Fat- 19 grams

➢ Carbs-37 grams

➢ Protein-17 grams

➢ Fiber-1.5 grams

Cheddar Biscuits

The ingredients for this recipe are as follows:

★ 2 cups of biscuit mix

★ A quarter cup of butter

★ ⅔ of a cup of milk

★ A single cup of mild cheddar cheese that is shredded

★ A quarter teaspoon of garlic powder

The steps to complete this recipe are as follows:

1. Heat your oven to 450 F.

2. Grease a baking sheet.

3. Mix the biscuit mix, milk, and cheese in a bowl. Make sure that the batter is doughy and soft. A wooden spoon will help with this, and it should take half a minute.

4. Put the batter on the sheet in spoonfuls.

5. Bake 10 minutes, and the biscuits should be a light brown.

6. Heat the garlic and butter in a pan on low heat until it is melted. This will take 5 minutes.

7. Brush that mix over the biscuits.

This recipe will take 20 minutes to complete.

Nutritional information (per serving):

➢ Calories-385

➢ Fat-24.6 grams

➢ Carbs-31.5 grams

➢ Protein-10.2 grams

Zucchini Bread

This recipe will need the following ingredients:

★ Half a teaspoon of baking powder

★ Half a teaspoon of all-purpose flour

★ Half a teaspoon of baking soda

★ Half a teaspoon of ground cinnamon

★ Half a cup of unsweetened applesauce

★ A single cup and a half of zucchini that has been lightly packed but not drained of liquid and grated

★ A single cup of granulated sugar

★ A quarter cup of packed brown sugar (light)

★ 2 eggs (large)

★ A single teaspoon of vanilla extract

★ A third of a cup of vegetable oil

You will need to complete the following steps:

1.   Heat your oven to 350 F.

2.   Get a 9 by 5 loaf pan and spray it with cooking spray.

3.   Get a bowl and add everything in but the baking powder, flour, and cinnamon along with the baking soda.

4.   Whisk all of these together until they have combined well.

5.   Add in the cinnamon and baking soda along with the flour and baking powder and stir until there is no dry flour remains. Do not over mix this, however.

6. Pour the batter in the pan and bake for 50 minutes. A toothpick should have moist crumbs on it.

7. Cool for 10 minutes.

8. Move to a cooling rack and let it cool totally.

This recipe will give you a dozen servings.

You will need an hour and 10 minutes to complete this recipe.

Nutritional information (per serving):

➢ Calories-213

➢ Carbs-35 grams

➢ Protein-3 grams

➢ Fat- 7 grams

Blueberry Pound Cake

The ingredients for this recipe are as follows:

★ 2 Tablespoons of butter

★ A quarter cup of white sugar

★ 2 ¾ cups of all-purpose flour

★ A single teaspoon of baking powder

★ A single cup of butter

★ 4 eggs

★ 2 cups of white sugar

★ 2 cups of blueberries that are fresh

★ A single teaspoon of vanilla extract

★ A quarter cup of flour that is all-purpose

The steps to complete this recipe are as follows:

1. Preheat your oven to 325 F.

2. Grease a pan that is 10 inches with 2 tablespoons of butter.

3. Sprinkle that same pan with a quarter cup of sugar.

4. Mix 2 ¾ of the cup of flour with the baking powder and place it to the side.

5. Get a bowl and cream a cup of butter and 2 cups of sugar together until it has become fluffy and light.

6. Beat the eggs one at a time before stirring the vanilla in.

7. Slowly beat in your flour mix.

8. Dredge your berries with the last quarter cup of flour.

9. Fold into the batter before pouring it in your prepared pan.

10. Bake for 80 minutes. The toothpick test should show a clean toothpick.

11. Let cool for 10 minutes into the pan before letting it totally cool on a wire rack.

This recipe will take you 90 minutes to finish.

Nutritional information (per serving):

➢ Calories-338

➢ Fat-14.5 grams

➢ Carbs-48.8 grams

➢ Protein-4.3 grams

Jam Pockets

The ingredients for this recipe are as follows:

★ A single teaspoon of vanilla

★ A single egg

★ 2 cups of flour

★ Half a cup of powdered sugar

★ A single cup of butter that is cut into cubes and cold

The steps to complete this recipe are as follows:

1. Preheat your oven to 375.

2. Use a food processor and combine your sugar and flour until they have mixed.

3. Toss in your butter and give it a few long buzzes with it until it has a cornmeal look.

4. Add the vanilla and egg and then buzz it twice more. You should be left with a soft dough.

5. Cover with plastic wrap and then let it chill in the fridge for a couple of hours.

6. Roll out our dough and use a cookie cutter to make circles.

7. Add the jam of your choice to the center and fold your edges inward. It should overlap in the middle.

8. Bake 10 minutes.

9. The bottom should be a faint brown color.

10. When cooled, sprinkle sugar over the top.

This recipe will give you 2 dozen pockets.

This recipe will take you 2 hours and 20 minutes to finish.

Croissants

The ingredients for this recipe are as follows:

★ A single cup of milk

★ 4 cups of flour that is all-purpose

★ A third of a cup of sugar that is granulated

★ 2 and a quarter teaspoons of salt that is kosher

★ 4 teaspoons of yeast that is active and dry

★ A cup and a quarter of butter that is cold and unsalted

★ An egg wash (this is to have a single large egg, and you beat it with a teaspoon of water)

The steps to complete this recipe are as follows:

1. Place your yeast and salt along with the flour and sugar in a bowl and whisk it all together until it has combined well.

2. Slice your butter into slices an eighth of an inch thick and toss it into the flour mix so that the butter is coated.

3. Add your milk in and stir it together. A stiff dough will be made.

4. Wrap your dough and make sure it's tight. You are going to use plastic wrap. Let it chill for 60 minutes.

5. Get yourself a lightly floured surface and roll your dough into a big and long rectangle.

6. Fold and make it like a letter. This means you fold it into thirds. Turn it 90 degrees and repeat 4 times.

7. The dough should be flat and smooth with streaks of butter in it.

8. Rewrap it again and chill for another 60 minutes. Divide the dough in half and then roll again.

9. It should be an eighth of an inch thick.

10. Cut your dough into triangles that are long and skinny.

11. Notch your wide end of each triangle you made with a half-inch cut.

12. Roll from the wide end to the end with a point. Tuck the point under the croissant.

13. Place on a baking sheet that is lined with parchment.

14. Cover with plastic wrap (loosely) and allow it to proof for 120 minutes.

15. Preheat your oven to 375 F.

16. Brush the croissants with your egg wash.

17. Bake 20 minutes.

18. They should be a puffy brown golden color, and they should be flaky.

This recipe will give you a dozen croissants.

This recipe will take you an hour to finish.

Nutritional information (per serving):

➤ Calories-294

➤ Fat-16 grams

➤ Protein- 5 grams

➤ Fiber- 1 gram

➤ Carbs-31 grams

Chapter 8: Baked Dessert Recipes

Chocolate Cake

This recipe will require the following ingredients:

★ 2 cups of white sugar

★ A cup and a 3/4 of flour that is all-purpose

★ 2 eggs

★ A single cup of milk

★ Half a cup of vegetable oil

★ ¾ of a cup of cocoa powder that has been unsweetened

★ A single teaspoon and a half of baking powder

★ A single teaspoon and a half of baking soda

★ 2 teaspoons of vanilla extract

★ A single cup of water that is boiling

The steps that you will need to take to complete this recipe is the following:

1. Heat the oven to 350 F.

2. Grease and flour 2 round pans that are 9 inches.

3. Get a bowl.

4. Mix everything in a bowl but the eggs, vanilla, and oil. Don't use the water yet either.

5. Stir everything together.

6. Add the oil, vanilla, and eggs, and the milk and mix for 2 minutes with a mixer on medium speed.

7. Stir in the water.

8. Pour in the pans.

9. Bake for a half-hour.

10. Cool for 10 minutes before you move to a wire rack.

This recipe will take you an hour to finish.

Nutritional information (per serving):

➢ Calories-157

➢ Fat-5.7 grams

➢ Carbs-25.7 grams

➢ Protein-2.3 grams

Blondies

This recipe will require the following ingredients:

★ A single cup of melted and unsalted butter

★ 2 and a half cups of flour that is all-purpose

★ 2 large eggs and a single egg yolk

★ A cup and a quarter of brown sugar that has been tightly packed

★ Half a cup of sugar

★ 2 teaspoons of vanilla extract

★ A single cup of walnuts that are chopped

★ ⅔ of a cup of white chocolate chips

★ Half of a teaspoon of baking powder

★ 2 teaspoons of cornstarch

The steps that you will need to take to complete this recipe is the following:

1. Preheat your oven to 350 F.

2. Line a 13 by 9 pan with parchment paper.

3. Combine your sugar and melted butter in a bowl.

4. Add your yolk, eggs, and vanilla extract and then stir until everything has been fully combined.

5. Set this to the side.

6. In another bowl, whisk your other ingredients together except the nuts and chocolate chips.

7. Then fold the nuts and chips in.

8. Put the batter in the pan.

9. Put it in the oven and bake for a half-hour.

10. Let cool.

This recipe will give you 15 servings.

This recipe will take you an hour to finish.

Nutritional information (per serving):

➢ Calories-370

➢ Fat-20 grams

➢ Carbs-46 grams

➢ Protein-4 grams

Carrot Cake

The ingredients you will need is the following:

★ 2 teaspoons of cinnamon that is ground

★ 2 cups of flour that is all-purpose

★ 2 cups of white sugar

★ 4 eggs

★ A single cup and a quarter of vegetable oil

★ 2 teaspoons of extract of vanilla

★ 2 teaspoons of baking soda

★ 2 teaspoons of baking powder

★ 3 cups of carrots that are grated

★ A single cup of pecans that are chopped

★ Half a cup of softened butter

★ A teaspoon of extract of vanilla

★ 4 cups of confectioner's sugar

★ 8 ounces of softened cream cheese

★ A single cup of pecans that are chopped

The steps you will need to take to complete this dish are as follows:

1. Heat your oven to 350.

2. Get a bowl and set it aside before you get a pan that is 9 by 13 and you grease and flour it.

3. Beat your eggs, vanilla, sugar, and oil together.

4. Mix in the baking powder and soda along with your cinnamon and flour.

5. Then stir in the carrots before you fold in your pecans.

6. Pour the mix in the pan that you prepared for the oven.

7. Bake for 50 minutes and then let cool for ten before you move it to a wire rack.

8. Let cool totally.

For the topping:

1. Get a bowl and combine everything before beating it. When it's creamy, add in the pecans that are chopped.

2. Put it on top.

This will take you two hours to complete.

Nutritional information (per serving):

➢ Calories-575

➢ Fat-34.8

➢ Carbs-63.7 grams

Chocolate Chip Cookies

This recipe will require the following ingredients:

★ A single cup of softened butter

★ 2 eggs

★ 2 teaspoons of vanilla extract

★ A single teaspoon of baking soda

★ A single cup of white sugar

★ A single cup of brown sugar that is packed

★ 2 cups of chocolate chips that are semi-sweet

★ 3 cups of all-purpose flour

★ A single cup of walnuts that are chopped

★ 2 teaspoons of hot water

The steps that you will need to take to complete this recipe is the following:

1. Heat the oven to 350 F.

2. Cream together the sugar and butter until it's smooth.

3. Beat in your eggs one at a time and stir in your vanilla.

4. Dissolve the baking soda in your hot water.

5. Add in the butter before stirring in the nuts and chips.

6. Drop spoonfuls onto a pan.

7. Bake 1o minutes.

This recipe will take you an hour to finish

Nutritional information (per serving):

➢ Calories-298

➢ Carbs-38.8 grams

➢ Fat-15.6 grams

➢ Protein-3.6 grams

Apple Pie

This recipe will require the following ingredients:

★ A quarter teaspoon of ground ginger

★ Half a cup of sugar

★ Half a cup of brown sugar that is packed

★ A single teaspoon of cinnamon that is ground

★ 3 tablespoons of flour that is all-purpose

★ A single tablespoon of lemon juice from a lemon

★ A single tablespoon of butter

★ A single, double-crust pie

★ Half a dozen tart apples that are sliced thinly

★ A single white large egg

★ A quarter teaspoon of nutmeg that is ground

The steps that you will need to take to complete this recipe is the following:

1. Get a bowl and combine the spices, flour, and sugars.

2. In another bowl, put in the lemon juice and toss the apples in it.

3. Add in the sugar mix and toss so they are coated.

4. Line the pie plate with bottom crust and trim so that it is even with the edge.

5. Fill it with the apple mix and dot with butter.

6. Roll the rest of the crust on top to fit the top.

7. Place it over the filling.

8. Trim before sealing and fluting the edges.

9. Cut slits into the crust.

10. Beat the egg white until it becomes foamy and brush it over that crust.

11. Place sugar over it.

12. Cover those edges with foil but do it loosely.

13. Bake for 25 minutes at a heat of 375.

14. Take off the foil and bake until the crust is a golden brown color and the filling is nice and bubbly.

15. This will take an additional 25 minutes.

16. Let it cool on a wire rack.

This recipe will give you eight servings.

This recipe will take you an hour and 20 minutes to finish.

Nutritional information (per serving):

➢ Calories-414

➢ Fat-16 grams

➢ Carbs-67 grams

Snickerdoodles

This recipe will require the following ingredients:

★ 2 eggs

★ Half of a cup of shortening

★ A half of a cup of softened butter

★ A cup and a half of white sugar

★ 2 teaspoons of cinnamon that is ground

★ 2 tablespoons of white sugar

★ 2 teaspoons of extract of vanilla

★ A single teaspoon of baking soda

★ 2 teaspoons of tartar (cream of tartar)

★ 2 ¾ cups of flour that is all-purpose

The steps that you will need to take to complete this recipe is the following:

1. Heat up your 400 F.

2. Cream the butter, sugar, eggs, vanilla, and shortening before blending in tartar, soda, and flour.

3. Shape your dough and put it into balls.

4. Mix up your sugar (the tablespoons) and cinnamon.

5. Roll your dough in that mix.

6. Bake 10 minutes.

7. Remove right away from the baking sheets.

This recipe will take you an hour to finish

Nutritional information (per serving):

➤ Calories-92

➤ Fat-4.3 gram

➤ Carbs-12.4 grams

Coffee Cake

This recipe will require the following ingredients:

For your topping:

★ A single cup of flour that is all-purpose

★ A single tablespoon and a half of cinnamon that is ground

★ A single cup of brown sugar that is light

★ Half a dozen tablespoons of melted butter

For the cake itself:

★ A single cup of sugar that is granulated

★ A single cup of room temperature butter

★ 3/4 of a cup of sour cream

★ 3 teaspoons of baking powder

★ ⅔ of a cup of brown sugar that is light

★ 3 eggs

★ A single tablespoon of vanilla extract

★ A single cup and a quarter of milk

★ 3 ⅔ cup of flour that is all-purpose

For the filling:

★ ¾ of a cup of flour that is all-purpose

★ 2 teaspoons of cinnamon that is ground

★ ¾ of a cup of brown sugar that is light

For the icing:

★ 2-3 tablespoons of milk

★ A single cup of powdered sugar

The steps that you will need to take to complete this recipe is the following:

1. Make sure that your oven is heated to 350 F.

2. Get a 9 by 13 baking dish and spray with nonstick spray.

3. Place to the side.

4. Get a bowl and whisk together the items for the filling before putting it to the side as well.

5. For the topping mix everything together in a bowl, and it should look like crumbs. Form pieces with your hands. Place to the side.

6. As for the cake, mix your sugar and butter in a bowl and use a mixer at medium speed for 120 seconds.

7. It should be fluffy and light.

8. You need to add in the sour cream, vanilla, eggs, and baking powder and mix for 60 seconds. It should be combined, and it should be smooth as well.

9. Put your mixer to a low setting and add in the milk and flour (alternating the portions) begin with the flour, end with the flour.

10. Mix until it is smooth and just combined.

11. Spread half of the batter in the pan and sprinkle the filling over the top. Then place the remaining batter on top.

12. Place the topping on top.

13. Bake for 45 minutes.

14. Remove from the oven and place on a wire rack.

15. Let it totally cool.

16. Drizzle the icing on top.

This recipe will give you a dozen servings.

This recipe will take you an hour and 5 minutes to finish.

Nutritional information (per serving):

➢ Calories-660

➢ Fat-24.9 grams

➢ Carbs-101.1 grams

➢ Protein-9.6 grams

Cheesecake

This recipe will require the following ingredients:

★ A single cup of sour cream

★ 2 Teaspoons of vanilla

★ 3 eggs

★ 3 (8 ounces) packages of softened cream cheese

★ A third of a cup of divided sugar

★ A third of a cup of melted butter

★ A cup and ¾ of graham cracker crumbs

★ A single can of cherry pie filling (go for 21 ounces)

The steps that you will need to take to complete this recipe is the following:

1. Heat your oven to 350.

2. Mix the crumbs, sugar and butter and press into a springform pan that is 9 inches.

3. Beat the cream cheese and leftover sugar using a mixer.

4. Mix until it is blended.

5. Add vanilla and sour cream, and make sure to mix it all well before adding in your egg. Go one at a time and beat it all on low speed.

6. Pour it over the crust.

7. Bake for 60 minutes.

8. You can top it with the filling.

Nutritional information (per serving):

➢ Calories-313

➢ Fat-17.7 grams

➢ Carbs-35.8 grams

Lemon Bars

This recipe will require the following ingredients:

★ A single cup of softened butter

★ A single cup and a half of white sugar

★ A quarter cup of all-purpose flour

★ Half a cup of white sugar

★ 2 juiced lemons

The steps that you will need to take to complete this recipe is the following:

1. Heat your oven to 350 F.

2. Get a bowl.

3. Blend half a cup of sugar and 2 cups of flour along with butter that has softened.

4. Get a 9 by 13 pan and press it into the bottom.

5. Bake 20 minutes.

6. Get a bowl.

7. Whisk a quarter cup of flour and a cup and a half of a cup of sugar.

8. Whisk in the lemon juice and the eggs.

9. Pour over the crust.

10. Bake another 20 minutes.

11. They will firm as they cool.

This recipe will take you an hour to finish

Nutritional information (per serving):

➢ Calories-126

➢ Fat-5.8 grams

➢ Carbs-17.8 grams

➢ Protein-1.6 grams

Made in the USA
Monee, IL
15 December 2020